READ ALL ABOUT IT!

Class N

e a

ANIMAL WELFARE

ADAM HIBBERT

2015

FRANKLIN WATTS
LONDON•SYDNEY

This edition 2004

First published in 2000 by Franklin Watts
96 Leonard Street, LONDON EC2A 4XD

Franklin Watts Australia
45-51 Huntley Street
NSW 2015

Copyright © Franklin Watts 2000 and 2004

Series editor: Rachel Cooke
Assistant editor Kate Newport
Designer: John Christopher, White Design
Picture research: Sue Mennell

A CIP catalogue record for this book is available from
the British Library.

ISBN 0 7496 5673 5

Dewey Classification 179

Printed in Malaysia

Acknowledgements:
Cartoons Andy Hammond pp 11, 15, 18, 23, 24;
Sholto Walker p 14.

Photographs Front cover: Rex Features: top right, centre
below (Peter Brooker); Holt Studios International: centre
above (Nigel Cattlin); Still Pictures: bottom right (José
Kalpers); RSPCA Photolibrary: bottom left (Robin Culley);
Back cover: RSPCA Photolibrary (Robin Culley); Inside:
Angling Times p. 29 t (Stuart Roper); Camera Press p. 16 t;
Patrick Douglas-Hamilton p. 20 b; Ronald Grant pp. 3 tc, 21 bl;
Heinz Frozen and Chilled Foods p. 22 t; Holt Studios
International pp. 8 t (Inga Spence), 18 (Nigel Cattlin);
Illustrated London News Picture Library p. 26; Impact Photos
p. 3 c (Otto/Visions); Frank Lane Picture Agency pp. 9
(Sunset/Jm Fichaux), 27 (John Watkins); Mayhew Animal
Home p. 29 b; Panos Pictures p. 11 (Guy Mansfield); Courtesy
of Quality Equipment p. 14; Rex Features pp. 6, 7 t, 7 b, 16 b
(Richard Jones), 19 (Peter Macdiarmid), 20 t (Peter
Brooker), 21 t (Charles Sykes), 28; RSPCA Photolibrary pp. 4,
5 b (Tom Claxton), 5 t (Colin Seddon), 13 b (Paul Herrmann),
17 (Ken McKay), 23 (Angela Hampton); Still Pictures pp. 3 tl
(Mark Edwards), 8 b (Mark Edwards), 10 t (Paul Glendell), 10
b (Evelyn Gallardo), 24 (José Kalpers), 25 (Mark Cawardine).

EDITOR'S NOTE

Read All About It: Animal Welfare takes the form of a newspaper called *The Animal News*. In it you can find a lot of articles about a lot of different subjects and many facts. It also includes opinions about these facts, sometimes obviously as in the editorial pages, but sometimes more subtly in a straight news article: for example in the article concerning the Exxon Valdez clean-up (page 10). Like any newspaper, you must ask yourself when you read the book 'What does the writer think?' and 'What does the writer want me to think?', as well as 'What do I think?'.

However there are several ways in which *The Animal News* is not and cannot be a newspaper. It deals with one issue rather than many and it has not been published on a particular day at a particular moment in history, with another version to be published tomorrow. While *The Animal News* aims to look at the major issues concerning animal welfare and animal rights today, the events

reported have not necessarily taken place in the past few days but rather over the past few years. They have been included because they raise questions that are relevant to the issue today and that will continue to be so in the future.

Another important difference is that *The Animal News* has been written by one person, not many, in collaboration with an editor. He has used different 'voices' and, in some instances, such as the letters and opinion pieces, pseudonyms (they are easy to spot!). However the people and events reported and commented on are real.

There are plenty of other things in *The Animal News* that are different from a true newspaper. Perhaps a useful exercise would be to look at the book alongside a real newspaper and think about, not only where we have got the approach right, but where we have got it wrong! In the meantime, enjoy reading *The Animal News*.

THE ANIMAL NEWS

ANIMALS FEEL PAIN! OFFICIAL!

The News Editor

A new study proves that animals can experience feelings of stress and pain. The findings are those of British biologist Professor Patrick Bateson, based on studies of muscle damage and 'stress' chemicals found in the bloodstream of deer hunted with hounds in Scotland. Bateson's results add fuel to the arguments against blood sports in Britain and elsewhere.

The report also has implications for several other industries that are presently accepted on the basis that animals do not feel stress. The use of animals in medical experiments, the

Hounds pursue a stag even when it swims a river.

battery-farming of chickens and even horse-racing could all be called into question.

Some scientists disagree with Prof. Bateson, saying his results do not prove anything about an animal's state of

mind. His claim that the chemicals he found are evidence of emotional distress is based on a comparison with similar chemicals in human bodies – his critics believe this comparison is unscientific. ∎

ARMY ABUSING ANIMALS?

Animal welfare groups are up in arms! They are furious because trainee surgeons in the Army have used live pigs to practise 'battlefield surgery'. According to a leaked army memo, the pigs were anaesthetised and shot at short range with powerful rifles. The trainees, on a special course in Denmark, used the injured pigs to improve their skill at repairing gunshot wounds. The army argues that such experience is vital for helping in civil conflicts such as Bosnia and Kosovo, where many civilians are injured by snipers. ∎

HUNTING: A GOOD SPORT?
READ MORE ON PAGE 27

SWAN SONG

Appeal launched as anglers are blamed for the rising death toll of one of our best-loved birds

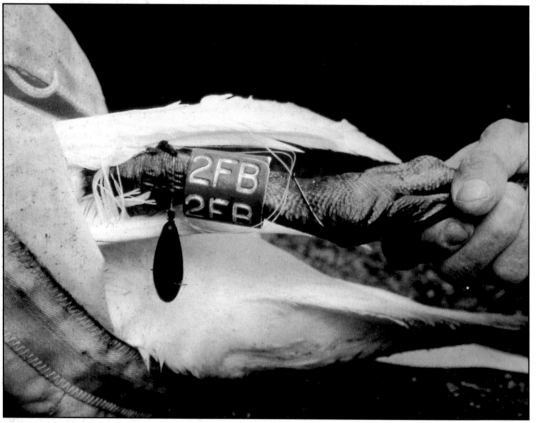

Luckily, help is at hand for this swan, whose leg has become tangled in fishing wire.

The swan population is suffering major losses because of careless fishermen, welfare groups warned today.

Home Affairs Editor

The National Convention for the Welfare of Swans and Wildlife, which operates 30 swan rescue centres across the country, has counted 720 fishing-related injuries in the first nine months of last year. The birds can be poisoned by the lead pellets used to weigh down bait, and strangled by lengths of discarded fishing line. An appeal was mounted for anglers to take more care when throwing away their old fishing tackle.

BAN IGNORED

The problem is a long-standing one. Legislation was introduced in 1987 which banned the sale of poisonous lead weights as fishing tackle. But after an initial drop in swan injuries, anglers appear to have returned to their previous bad habits. Swan injuries have steadily increased ever since. Apart from tackle, waterfowl are threatened by other human refuse. The plastic ties on four-pack cans of beer litter our canals and rivers, thrown away by careless revellers. These apparently harmless ties strangle an uncounted number of birds each year.■

FEELING CHIPPER!

The government is to examine ways to encourage dog and cat owners to have a microchip ID tag injected into their beloved pet. Almost a million pet owners have voluntarily taken-up private identity chips offered by vets, which help in the return of missing pets to their owners.

Chips are welcomed by animal welfare groups, who recognise that a permanent link between animal and owner makes it harder to get away with abusing or abandoning pets. Theft and loss of prized pets can also be prevented by the permanent chip, which is typically injected into the nape of the animal's neck.

The April 2001 change in the law introducing pet passports is likely to lead to a further uptake of chipping. Passports use microchip IDs and vet's records to confirm that a pet is properly inoculated for travel to and from countries where rabies can be caught. Pet owners in Britain can then take their animals to Europe, on holiday or to show in competitions. ■

Market confusion as free-range products come home to roost

Chicken-friendly shoppers

Free-range

Despite claims to the contrary from egg-producers, consumers appear to be deserting cheap battery-farmed eggs in favour of more chicken-friendly products. Compassion in World Farming (CIWF), the international animal welfare group, has found that free-range and barn-raised eggs account for almost half of supermarket sales.

SHELL SHOCKED

The results were received with surprise in Britain, where over 80% of egg-laying chickens are farmed in battery cages. The British Egg Information Service, representing major egg producers, claimed that 'many people say they want the choice of free-range, but when it comes to shopping, they buy eggs from the laying cage [battery eggs] because they are cheaper'.

This discrepancy may be because consumers are clearly confused. A recent National Opinion Poll discovered that nearly 40% of consumers assumed that the words 'farm fresh' on the box meant that the eggs were free-range.

Philip Lymbery of CIWF believes that supermarkets are partly to blame for this confusion as they will sometimes price battery eggs at the higher, free-range price. They also use similar packaging for the battery eggs, and position them alongside the actual free-range eggs.

The statistics are also biased by the fact that consumers only buy a fraction of all eggs produced. The remaining eggs are bought and used by caterers, restaurants and food processing companies. Labelling rules do not require processed foods or restaurant menus to announce whether egg ingredients are from free-range or battery farms. ■

Eggs in your basket

Free-range eggs are from chickens allowed to roam in large, outdoor enclosures. It is the most costly farming and is thought by many to be kinder to chickens, but there is evidence that free-range chickens are more exposed to diseases.

Barn-raised eggs are from roaming chickens in roofed enclosures. Barn-raised farming combines some of the cost advantages of battery-farming with some of the ethical advantages of free-range farming.

Battery-farmed eggs are from chickens kept indoors in small wire cages. This method is cheapest of all, but confines chickens to small spaces and there is evidence the chickens experience stress. ■

Battery-farmed

Would you take on this dog? Some simple home improvements might make all the difference to your decision...

A Make-Over for Kennels

IN THE DOG HOUSE

An estimated 1,000 dogs are abandoned in Britain every day. Several hundred more are handed-in by pet owners who are moving to another country, or who can no longer cope with their pet, typically for health reasons. Dog welfare groups find and house these dogs, nursing the sick and elderly ones, and trying to find them 'foster parents' as an alternative to being put down. ■

Research presented yesterday to the Psychological Society Conference promises to make tails wag – just by giving a little extra care to interior design. The research into 120 stray dogs, presented by Dr Deborah Wells of Queen's University, Belfast, found that certain dogs in animal rescue shelters behaved in ways which were off-putting to potential new owners.

Dogs which barked too much, or which lay down at the back of the cage and ignored visitors, were themselves ignored by people on the look-out for a rescued pet. Without a home to go to, most of these unwanted strays have to be put down by shelters after a few weeks.

By making minor changes to the dogs' environment, such as moving the dog's basket further forward and tying a chewing toy to the front of the cage, Dr Wells found that the animals' behaviour improved, making 'a more favourable impression, which has increased the number of dogs that have been purchased from the shelters'. ■

Protesters' Rights

Animal welfare demonstrators worried by new rules extending police powers

Animal activists and civil rights campaigners reacted with anger and dismay to a new police initiative to monitor their campaigns. Speaking up for demonstrators at British ports attempting to stop the export of live animals, John Callaghan of Compassion in World Farming said 'This is going too far. We are constantly being videoed by the police – I'm worried as a law-abiding person that we are coming under this kind of scrutiny. Peaceful demonstration is part of a democratic society – it is part of our rights'.

A police spokesperson defended the new unit – 'if you know that certain groups are involved in an action, you can anticipate greater disorder ... and plan for it in advance'. The bill for policing demonstrations against live animal exports at ports in Britain in 1995 was in excess of £6 million.

It was at this time that live animal export first really came to public attention. Calves were enduring very unhealthy conditions in transit to European farms and abbatoirs. Drivers of cattle trucks were often unaware of the calves' need for rest and watering, and several calves in each load were often found dead by random inspections. Protests led to stronger regulations and conditions improved in the UK. But there are still concerns about transport conditions on mainland Europe. ■

Protesters make their feelings clear in Plymouth.

DAMAGES FOR PROTESTER

A 53-year old protester, Angela Petro, was awarded £10,000 in damages from Kent police for their treatment of her at demonstrations against live animal exports. She had claimed wrongful arrest and imprisonment on three occasions, involving strip searches and injury to her wrists. ■

THE COST OF KINDNESS?

Animal rescue centres in Britain are having to cope with thousands of abandoned male calves. As a result of protests against live export and latterly the BSE crisis, farmers can no longer export the calves for veal, and face large bills for disposing of the unwanted cattle. The dairy industry only needs female cows for milk. ■

FARMING IN CRISIS? SEE PAGE 19

An animal activist is reluctantly led away by police.

MAFIA BEEF

A Belgian government meat inspector has been murdered. **Karel Van Noppen,** who headed Belgium's campaign against the illegal use of hormones to enhance beef production, was shot a few steps from his front door. The gunman is thought to have been working for the Belgian mafia. The Belgian government reacted swiftly to the murder, imposing tough controls and spot checks.

Mrs Van Noppen said that her husband had received several threats to cease his investigations into the illegal supply and use of hormones. Relatively simple to manufacture, hormones are injected into cattle, stimulating muscle growth and massively improving farmers' profits per animal. But concerns over the possible side-effects on people who eat hormone-treated beef meant their use was banned in the European Union in 1989. Now hormones are supplied to farmers illegally via a mafia-dominated black market.

Welfare groups argue that, whatever the risk to humans, the use of hormones is cruel to animals. Poultry and pigs are often deformed by the drug, and cattle can experience heart problems. However, hormones are not banned in North America or Australia, where their routine use results in significantly cheaper meat for consumers. ■

Fat, healthy US cattle? Or hormone-boosted meat?

DEAD DOGS TO FEED THE HOMELESS

Foreign Affairs Editor

The people of the impoverished Mexican city of Puebla, in particular the homeless, are to benefit from a ground-breaking animal welfare scheme. In a bid to reduce the numbers of stray dogs in the city, public health officials are offering a food parcel in exchange for every stray dog handed in.

The dogs, which suffer from malnutrition and often carry distemper, rabies and dangerous parasites, will be humanely put down by health officials. Domestic pet diseases will be reduced as a result. Jesus Loreno Aarun, Health Secretary for the region, defended the scheme, noting that funds were not available to catch and neuter the estimated 900,000 strays. ■

This Mexican boy will need to take extra care of his puppy!

Dog disposal outrage

Letters of protest have been flooding in to **Miyazaki Prefecture in Kyushu, Japan,** following a television programme which revealed that the city dog pound had installed a chute for depositing stray dogs, outside the pound's regular opening hours. ■

Bullfighting in the dock

Private bull-fighting party like a red rag to a bull for Nîmes prosecutor

Denis Lore, France's premier bullfighter, faces trial with nine others for cruelty to animals. Bullfighting is contrary to French animal cruelty laws, but in southern cities where the sport has a long history, local exemptions apply to particular bull rings.

NO CORRIDA?

Mr Lore stands accused of helping to organise a private 'bullfighting party' at a farm near one such exempted city, Nîmes. Maitre Jean-Jacques Pons, the torero's lawyer, said that the case was crucial to the future of La Corrida, the style of bullfighting that results in the death of the bull.

Josyane Querelle, leader of a federation of anti-bullfighting groups, was optimistic: 'If a bullfighter is convicted of cruelty to animals – something which has never happened anywhere in the world – it would be enormously important psychologically.'

NO WOMEN?

Whilst some fight to end bullfighting, others are fighting to take part. In 1996, Christina Sanchez was the

A bull is impaled with a long lance as it charges a mounted bullfighter.

first woman to achieve Matador status – the highest rank in bullfighting. Spanish feminists were jubilant. If women could conquer this macho part of Spanish culture, there could be no more dismissing of women's potential. ■

PAPAL BULL

Pope Pius V issued an order in 1567 that any Christian shown to have practised bullfighting was to be excommunicated – expelled from the church – which was as bad as a prison sentence. Pius found bullfighting to be 'contrary to Christian duty and piety' and 'more appropriate for devils than for men'. The Church has never withdrawn the order. ■

The slow road to recovery

Prince William Sound experienced one of the world's worst oil spills in 1989, when supertanker Exxon Valdez ran aground. Over a decade later, local wildlife and human inhabitants are still counting the cost.

This Arctic region attracts migrating whales, seals, sea otters and hundreds of bird species. But overnight in 1989, 1,500 miles of coastline was coated in a layer of oil, up to a foot thick in places. Just 7% of the 11 million gallons of oil spilled was ever recovered by clean-up crews. As a result, of the 17 species listed as threatened by the disaster, just two have recovered to their previous numbers: the bald eagle and river otter.

In 1994, Exxon was ordered to compensate 14,000 local fishermen and others to the tune of $5 billion; the company's appeal against the order is still being fought as we go to press. It seems likely that locals will eventually be paid for their loss – but for the hundreds of thousands of dead fish, birds, whales, seals, otters and crustaceans nothing can repair the damage. If just a little more time and money had been devoted to safety back in 1989, the story could have been very different. ■

THE PRICE OF INEXPERIENCE

A smaller spill at Milford Haven, Wales, in 1994 was found to have been caused by an employee of the port, leading the courts to impose a £4 million exemplary fine on the port's management trust. Ports send out 'pilots' to steer large ships in to dock, but the pilot sent to the Sea Empress was inexperienced and had not moved a large ship at low tide. The Sea Empress ran aground, spilling oil into the marine nature reserves of the Gower peninsula. ■

Oil spills make images of birds like this all too familiar.

Fire destroys rainforest

Up to a million hectares of the world's most biodiverse rainforest have gone up in flames since 1997. The forest, in the Kalimantan and Sumatran regions of Indonesia, has been suffering for years as a result of logging activity.

Clearing by loggers has allowed sunshine to dry the forest floor, turning it into nothing less than peat bricks and tinder wood, so fires can easily get out of control. Volunteer crews concentrate on evacuating people – and the occasional animal – from the choking smog. Twenty-nine orphaned orang utans were retrieved during the blaze in 1997. The forest is home to 12% of the world's mammal species, 16% of its reptiles and 17% of its birds. The last 400 Sumatran tigers are even more seriously threatened.

Although using fire to clear woodlands is officially banned, in practice the Indonesian government has made little effort to enforce controls. With some senior politicians having financial interests in logging companies, some groups feel that the government is only paying lip-service to environmental concerns. ■

Forest fires threaten the orang utan population.

GM animal organ donors

Scientists researching the possible use of pig cells and organs in human patients are making steady progress, despite public fears about the issues involved.

The shortage of organs from human donors is set to grow. Advances in road safety and casualty room medicine mean that the supply of suitable organs is shrinking. At the same time, medical advances make more illnesses curable with transplants.

Pig organs are not naturally accepted by human patients who need replacement kidneys, hearts, lungs or livers. But pig organs are the right size, and our long history of farming pigs makes them a predictable source of organs.

Recent advances include more reliable ways to create 'transgenic' pigs. These pigs carry a small piece of human DNA which tags their cells with a human protein. The protein tells a human patient's immune system not to attack the pig organ.

Stem cell research is also advancing. Political decisions to limit research on human stem cells – which must be harvested from human embryos – mean that animal alternatives are more heavily researched. In December 2002, scientists at University College, London (UK) announced that they had successfully grown new kidneys inside mice, using stem cells from pig embryos. ■

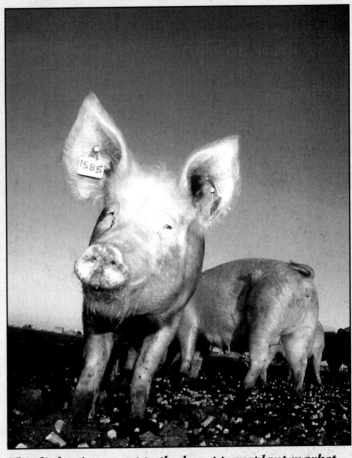

This little piggy went to the heart-transplant market...

Top Dogs?

A Californian couple have received counselling after suffering from 'Pack Position Confusion'. The couple, who had become timid and subservient to their pet Maltese dogs, were advised to growl and bark at their pets to reassert their position in the household. ■

BARK!!
BARK!!
BARK!!
BARK!!
GROWL
BARK
BARK!
BARK
BARK!!
BARK!
BARK!

Not just Christmas

Andrew Deller, manager of New Zealand's Telegraph and Telephone Company, had good news for pet-owning employees this year. 'A dog or a cat can be just as much of a dependant as a sick child', he explained, announcing a new policy to allow employees time off (with pay) to care for a sick pet. ■

Chop and change?

Teachers disagree over the use of dissection in the classroom

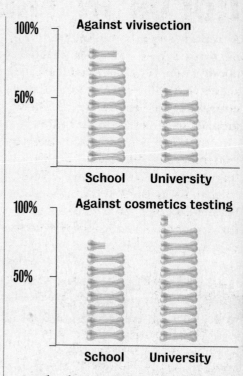

Against vivisection

100%

50%

School   University

Against cosmetics testing

100%

50%

School   University

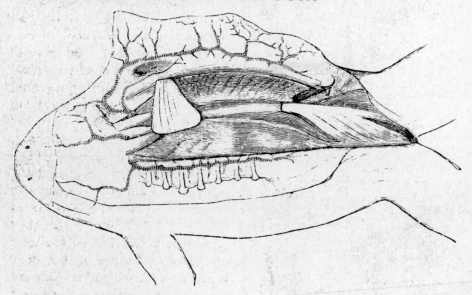

A diagram of a dissected frog reveals its heart and arteries.

A new study has found that one third of biology teachers are still using dissection as part of their coursework, following moves by the education authorities in the mid-90s to make it voluntary. Until campaigners lobbied the government to have it removed, many schools forced pupils to take part in dissections, sometimes despite their religious or ethical objections.

Jan Creamer of the National Anti-

The Education Correspondent

Vivisection Society (NAVS) was pleased with the progress so far, saying that 'it was a tremendously successful campaign'. But there was still much to be done to convince some biology teachers that alternative methods are more appropriate. Some still believe that the best way to learn about biology is by seeing for yourself. ■

Older & Wiser?

A comparison of attitudes to animal use between school and university students has found interesting differences. The survey, by Liverpool University, found that 83% of school students oppose vivisection, compared with just 57% at university.

Before you jump to the conclusion that older students are less caring, read on: it turns out that more undergraduates are opposed to the use of animals for testing cosmetics (91% compared to 75%).

Researchers have concluded that older students make more complex judgements about the issue. Undergraduates are more likely to accept animal experiments as 'necessary suffering' if the benefits – say, an AIDs cure – are worthwhile.

On the other hand, they are more likely to condemn cosmetics testing on animals if the benefits are frivolous – making a lipstick just that bit glossier, for example. For teenagers, improvements in cosmetics (e.g. spot cover-up creams) are more likely to be deemed worthwhile. ■

RSPCA IN THE CLASSROOM

A report recently highlighted the need for schools to teach children about animal welfare and care. It seems that children who receive this education are less likely to abuse animals in their care later in life.

In the light of this, it is worth remembering the great wealth of learning resources already offered to schools by the RSPCA. Alongside leaflets like the ones shown below, the society produces photocopiable Wildlife Worksheets, Action for Animals activity packs, Wildlife Gardens and a Good Practice handbook to help schools and children maintain the best standards in care for animals.

Many of these invaluable resources are available for free! You can find loads of information on their website as well, so why not check it out? For details see our Who's Who on page 30. ■

Children discuss animal welfare issues in school with help from the RSPCA.

Susie Roar's
Facts of Life

THERE WAS A TIME when one could keep a tortoise with no more resources than a cardboard box stuffed with straw and the occasional reminder from Blue Peter to move the beast in or out of said luxury accommodation.

My fond childhood memories of a tortoise called Hurry led me to believe that my own two children might benefit from a similar pet. How wrong I was!

On arrival at the pet shop, things rapidly went downhill. The price of a sustainably-bred tortoise made me gasp, I admit, but I'm not against good practice in the pet trade, so I lumped it.

Then came the shocker. Despite my childhood expertise, and not to mention that – as a mother – I have reared two well-adjusted young humans, after a few questions I was informed that I am not fit to be in possession of a tortoise. I was stunned.

I am much more responsible than I was aged five. Has animal welfare become such dogma that no child can ever again learn from its mistakes as a pet owner? Must every pitfall in life be ironed out by the authorities, before children have had a chance to figure it out for themselves? Pets may suffer a little in the process, but if we don't let children take these small steps alone, we will be creating a generation incapable of responsibility. That's when animals – and humans – will really start to suffer. ■

Editorial

ONCE MORE UNTO THE BREACH!

The turn of a new millennium is a good time to look back at what we've achieved, and at what we've failed to achieve, to discover what the next thousand years should deliver. But for animal welfare, there is no thousand or two thousand year track record. Almost all the advances we have made were won in the last 50 years. Animal welfare was born a mere two centuries ago, with the foundation of the RSPCA and sister organisations.

In some ways, we should take heart from this brief tale: so much has been achieved, in such a very short time (See **The Long March**, page 26). It is now no longer acceptable, in the Western world, to abuse a pet animal. It is increasingly unacceptable to treat farm and wild animals inhumanely (though this certainly still happens). And of course, our concern for the survival of other species has dramatically affected the way we arrange our economic activities.

We have won significant improvements for animals in our care, but should that be all we hope for? Should we turn our attention to the sort of goals supported by Frieda Fox in today's **Let's Discuss This?** Should gorillas be protected by something approaching human rights? Or should we maintain the steady course charted over the last 200 years? Ultimately, only the younger generations can decide.

DIFFERENT WORLDS

This week's news from abroad confirms the existence of very different attitudes towards animals in the many cultures of the world. It is all too easy to become bullish about a foreign country's 'cruelty' to various creatures. But proceed with caution. The idea of animal welfare we have developed in the West over the last two centuries is not necessarily right, and surely cannot be forced on everyone. Indeed, could it not be the case that these cultures have something to teach us? ■

Letters

Pig Necessities

As recipients of a lottery grant, we at City Farm have had to deal with a lot of uninformed media heckling over the installation of snout-operated showers for our pigs. The showers are not a novelty item; pigs are very tidy animals, and must have access to washing facilities to ensure their basic well-being. We hope that message will be heard by anyone who read the ridiculous nonsense in the press last week.
Derek Trotter

Just a quick shower...

Stop the fight

Bullfighting is recognised as a cruel entertainment, and is banned in several countries around the world, including my home state Arizona.

Now we hear of one Mario de la Fuente trying to set up a new bullring in Nogales, Mexico, just miles from the border with Arizona, which would rely on American tourist dollars to be viable.

Please don't let him get away with it. You can write to the Mayor of Nogales at: Avenida Obregon, Numero 395, Palacio Municipal, Nogales, Sonora, Mexico.
Hermione Noble

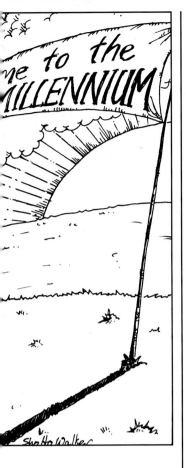

Let's discuss this

Bee Nicer
Vet and animal rescue volunteer

Animal welfare means caring for suffering animals and working to prevent the infliction of suffering on animals by humans. Animal welfare is not based on any single ideal other than sympathy for our fellow creatures, and perhaps our duty to be caring beings. Animal welfare is promoted by caring for individual animals, educating the public to treat animals better, and advising governments on welfare issues to win changes in the law.

Frieda Fox
Animal rights activist

Animal rights supporters recognise animals as our equals, rather than as tools humans may use and discard as we see fit. The idea of animal rights comes from the observation that animals are beings that can feel pain and suffering, and that it is human prejudice to rank our desires as more important than an animal's pain. Only by recognising these facts in legal rights for animals will they be freed from oppression.

Bee Nicer versus Frieda Fox

Dear Frieda,

If you really care about animals, you should devote your spare time to helping animal welfare charities such as the RSPCA.

The campaign for animal rights attacks those who use animals, by necessity or through choice. But these are just the people who need to be taught to care for their animals' welfare. All civilised human beings are against cruelty. I believe that, for our own moral well-being, it is in our interests to treat animals with dignity.

Yours,
BN

Dear Bee,

You talk of 'our own moral well-being'. But we're here to discuss what's in the animal's best interests, not our own.

Your approach turns us from talking about the needs of animals to a discussion entirely devoted to what's best for people – if that's not missing the point, I'm a monkey's uncle.

The point is that 'civilised' people don't even recognise that animals have every bit as much of a right to life as they do.

Yours,
FF

Dear Frieda,

In the absence of an animal parliament, at which farmyard animals discuss and vote on their own affairs, all talk of animal interests must be from a human viewpoint – it is dishonest of you to suggest that the animals would side with your argument.

From the human viewpoint, it makes sense to treat cruelty to animals as an insult to human dignity, to prevent it, to punish it, and to care for its victims.

With animal rights, as Bertrand Russell put it, you're arguing for 'votes for oysters'. It won't happen, nor should it.

Yours,
BN

Dear Bee,

I am not against animal welfare work – it does go some way towards redressing the balance. But you only ever treat the tip of the iceberg. While welfare organisations rescue a few tens of thousands of animals in Britain each year, three million animals are used in lab experiments!

Of course taking another being's life for our selfish purposes is wrong! But you're arguing from the viewpoint of a nurse who treats wounded soldiers, where I'm campaigning to stop the war.

Yours,
FF

Tally Ho!

Do your anti-hunting correspondents (Letters, last week) all live like monks? Everyone in this country benefits to some extent from the exploitation of animals.

Either it's killing animals that they object to, or it's the thrill of the hunt that these people hate, in which case they should admit to their prudishness.

For the undecided, consider living in a way that does not involve harming animals: no transport quicker than 8kph, sponges strapped to your feet and gauze over your mouth, and that's just to save some insects from accidental harm. Fine for monks, perhaps, but not for me!
name and address supplied

Circus Giant

Rolf Knie at work, 1944.

Obituary: Rolf Knie

Rolf Knie – animal-friendly Circus Giant – 1921-1997

Born to a fourth-generation Swiss circus family in 1921, Rolf Knie inspired the European circus industry for 50 years, directing the Circus Knie with his brother, Freddy, and training elephants to a world-beating standard.

Rolf started his circus career as a child acrobat, but grew too large so that the only course left open to him was to follow in his father's footsteps as a trainer of bears, horses and dogs. He presented his first elephant display at the age of 16 and never looked back.

Rolf pioneered the breeding of elephants in captivity, achieving several successes with Asian elephants. He also led the field in animal welfare, throwing his training programmes open to public viewing from 1939 onwards, to prove that no cruelty was involved. Many circuses with performing animals have followed his example throughout the world, helping live animals acts remain a part of the circus despite continuing pressure from some welfare groups.

The Knie family circus grew to become the Swiss National Circus and the Knie brothers were treated like minor royalty wherever they performed. In 1997 Rolf and other members of the Knie family were added to the International Circus Hall of Fame. His first son, Louis, has established a new circus in Austria. Rolf is succeeded by his second son, Franco, as director of the Swiss National Circus. ■

Profile: Panda man

Liu Xuefeng has a most unusual job. He is one of the very few people in the world who knows how to hand-rear the cubs of the giant panda.

On September 25th, 1998, Peking Zoo's giant panda female, Le Le, gave birth to two male cubs, weighing a tiny 180 grams each. Liu Xuefeng was one of the team that was rapidly assembled to ensure that the twins survived to adulthood.

Pandas are not very accomplished mothers. The smallest cubs are often abandoned or accidentally crushed by their giant parent, and zoos have often attempted to ensure success by removing one of a pair of cubs and hand-rearing it away from the female. Sadly, this is rarely successful.

Liu Xuefeng has been helping with a new approach. Rather than removing one cub permanently, his team swaps the cubs around every 12 hours. Each cub spends 12 hours with its mother, and 12 with a human nanny, such as Mr Liu.

'When being fed by hand,

Le Le and one of her cubs feeding on bamboo.

the cubs like to be hugged,' he says but adds, 'The cubs can fool around, and sometimes they scratch me.' ■

Diary: a day in the life of an animal rescue supervisor

Sarah Jones works as a supervisor for an animal rescue centre on the outskirts of Nottingham. She made a record for *The Animal News* of a typical day at the centre.

9am

Off to the hospital to collect a 10-month old Great Dane, whose had his legs pinned after a car accident. We're great friends already and he's happy to see me.

10am

Doing the rounds. The six care assistants fill me in on our trickier cases; need to get the visiting vet to check on Molly, a cat still limping after an operation. Just enough time to see how our new guinea pig is settling in; he's asleep in the corner of the hutch with his new friends.

10.30am

Back to the office to talk with Helen, the deputy manager. We're facing a bit of a cat crisis, exceeding our licence at one point this summer, with 180 cats in our care. A media appeal helped, but we're still having to turn cats away.

11.15am

Planning to cope is constantly interrupted with distraught phone calls. Tell one teenager to come in after lunch; she's crying, saying that her dad has threatened to drown five kittens if she doesn't find them a home today.

Dog walking is a welcome break in a supervisor's busy day.

12pm

Quick stockcheck; make a note to order more rabbit food. We're into viewing hours, and several visitors need a quick pointer or a bit of information.

12.40pm

Read up on new inmates in the cat kennels. Some have to be given quite odd names to avoid confusion; twenty cats called Mittens would soon have us scratching our heads.

1pm

Quick sandwich, and a walk for the Great Dane. I'm calling him Cody.

2pm

Try to keep the peace as an argument breaks out in reception over who is responsible for the fee for neutering a woman's unwanted cat. Cat and two kittens kept in for a check.

2.30pm

An inspector arrives with three adult stray cats and eight kittens. Each has to be checked for parasites, vaccinated for flu and enteritis, and recorded for the files.

3.40pm

Dying for a coffee to keep me going, but there's a man at reception who is emigrating and can't take his cat with him.

4.30pm

Visiting hours are over, and it's time for another check around the kennels. Volunteers take the dogs for a good long walk.

5pm

Round up the loose cats from the garden and pop them back in their kennels. Bed down the rabbits and guinea pigs.

6pm

I'm tired now, but there's one more task – draw up the staff rota for tomorrow. Then home for a quiet moment in front of the telly with my four cats. Bliss.

I'm always exhausted at the end of the day, but I wouldn't swap my job for the world. It's so important to me that animals in terrible circumstances get a fair chance. I try not to get angry with the people that cause animals suffering. Normally they have just under-estimated the responsibilities involved. Too many pet shops and breeders fail to check that owners really understand what they're getting into. But sometimes I have to wonder what goes through people's heads when they neglect or abandon their pet. My cats remind me not to get too cynical, though! ■

MALARIA THREAT TO AFRICAN ECONOMY

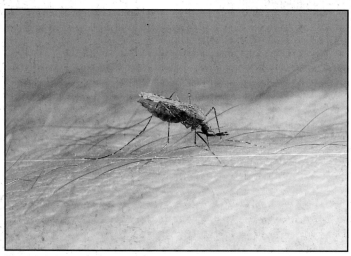

Malaria is transmitted to humans by mosquito bites.

Businesses in southern African countries, not least South Africa, are growing concerned at a United Nation's sponsored drive to ban the use of the anti-malaria insecticide, DDT (dichlorodiphenyltri-chloroethane).

Malaria already costs South Africa somewhere in the region of $50 million per year in lost work days and healthcare.

Malaria has killed more people than all the wars in history. DDT was first used as an insecticide by the Swiss Paul Müller at the beginning of World War II. He used it as a clothes-moth repellent, but it was soon used to control fleas, lice, mosquitos and certain crop pests. In the 1940s, the Italian city of Naples was saved from a lice-borne typhus epidemic by the chemical.

The UN objections to DDT date back to an ambitious mosquito 'eradication' pro-gramme in the 1950s. DDT was sprayed liberally on any potential malaria hot-spot, destroying other insect populations and building up in lethal doses higher up the food chain. In books such as *Silent Spring* by Rachel Carson, animal welfare and environmental experts condemned DDT for poisoning endangered predators and birds of prey.

But for four decades DDT use has been confined largely to spraying interior walls of houses, where only mosquitos are likely to be harmed. House-spraying has effectively controlled the disease in several tropical countries and reduced malarial territory in South Africa by 80%.

BITES BACK

Alternatives to DDT are more expensive, as is drug treatment for malaria sufferers. As a result, countries already pressured into banning DDT have suffered serious outbreaks of the disease. The only business to benefit from this process to date are those selling expensive DDT alternatives. Once again developing countries are faced with the difficulties of reconciling animal welfare and environmental concerns with the realities of business and commerce. ■

The Internet Investor

The Animal News finance editor gives his tips for joining the rush to invest in Internet-led business. But be warned, it is a dog-eat-dog world and there are as many losers as winners!

Web walkies!

The Internet is all about young urban professionals exchanging cutting-edge information on computer technology and Nike trainers, right? Wrong! Today's virtual millionaires are the ones who spot opportunities arising as more and more people turn on the computer. As the mass market arrives, so do previously under-represented consumer groups – pet owners, for example. Here's just a few of a pack of providers for our furry friends:

■ www.petsdirectuk.com is a no-nonsense supplier of food, treats, toys, travel accessories, books and even music CDs for your pampered pooches and purr-fect companions.
■ www.petsmart.com does for the American pet business what amazon.com did for books, with the added back-up of 600 superstores across the USA and Canada. Website offers chatty articles as well as catalogue details.

■ www.petplanet.co.uk is a more 'community-driven' site with plenty of forums, pet advice, breed information and other useful animal-lovers' resources, alongside an on-line shopping facility.
■ www.ukpets.co.uk
is a massive directory of pet resources around the UK, from shops to sitters. It also carries latest news stories for animal lovers about pet care, welfare groups and other relevant stories. ■

Farm workers disinfecting farm buildings during the Foot and Mouth disease outbreak in 2001.

Farming in the Doghouse

Future for small farmers looks bleak after another huge drop in farm incomes

The Finance Editor

UK farmers have been through a lot in the last ten years. First came the bans on beef sales due to the BSE epidemic. Then came the Foot & Mouth disease outbreak in 2001. This resulted in the destruction of 4.9 million sheep, 700,000 cattle and 400,000 pigs. Throughout this period, prices for cereals and milk products have fallen, in some cases to below the production cost.

For those farmers who survived this painful period, especially the larger businesses, it might have seemed that things could only get better. But changes to the global farming market may have more nasty surprises in store.

First comes the problem of the European Union (EU). With the expansion of the Union from 15 to 25 member countries in 2004, the grants made by the EU to its farmers had to be changed. This promises years of changing rules and red tape for farmers who rely on their grants.

Secondly, even if the EU's own plans for supporting farmers works, they may still face a further challenge from world trade. The USA, the EU and Japan make large grants, or subsidies, to their own farmers. The subsidy has various side effects, such as higher costs of food to consumers, and a surplus of food that is 'dumped' in the poor world, thus undermining farmers there.

In previous World Trade Organisation (WTO) talks, poor countries agreed to delay dealing with the problem until the end of 2003. In 2003, new WTO member China joined India, Brazil and 18 other developing countries to prepare their opposition. This 'G21' group of countries represents over half the world's population, the majority of them small farmers.

Will farmers in the wealthy world ride out this latest challenge? Or is it time for the majority to pack up and find new uses for their land? Only time will tell. ■

Concert Triumph

The Arts Reviewer

Yuki Matsuzawa, the Japanese concert pianist, was joined by the English Chamber Orchestra Ensemble for a stirring performance of works by Schubert and Chopin at the Wigmore Hall last night. The concert was in aid of the Japan Animal Welfare Society (JAWS).

Miss Matsuzawa's strengths lie in her complete command of the Chopin Etudes. She completed the first half of the concert with a sparkling selection, confirming her reputation as 'most exciting newcomer'. It also showed her dedication to the cause of animal welfare. ■

Beauty who loves the beasts! Pamela receives award.

Rising young star Yuki Matsuzawa at the piano.

PeTA awards

The stars came out in their hundreds to applaud winners at Hollywood's annual animal-lovers' awards, held by People for the Ethical Treatment of Animals (PeTA). As with many charitable concerns, celebrity backing is a great source of publicity for PeTA's cause and events like this also give a welcome boost to donations. Stars with a close association to the group include Richard Gere, David Duchovny, Woody Harrelson, Alicia Silverstone and Ellen DeGeneres.

But the belle of the ball was undoubtedly the winner of the Linda McCartney Memorial Award – the Baywatch beauty, Pamela Anderson Lee. The world's favourite blonde was pleased to prove that it's not what people think of you, 'it's what you do that counts'.

Held on the Paramount Studios lot, the ceremony included music from the B-52s, Chrissie Hynde and Sir Paul McCartney. There was also a tearful tribute to the late Linda McCartney, who was famous for her love of animals and promotion of their welfare. ■

Paralysed actor fights on

Christopher Reeve, the actor best known for his portrayal of Superman, is leading the charge into medical research to cure spinal injuries. Reeve was paralysed from the neck down after a riding accident in 1995, but has vowed to walk again.

Christopher Reeve, active campaigner for research into spinal injuries.

If a cure is to be found in the forseeable future, experiments on animals will have to happen. His campaign thus poses ethical difficulties for other Hollywood celebrities caught between their support for the disabled and their rejection of animal experimentation. AIDS campaigners caused similar worries in the 90s when they raised the importance of animal research to finding a cure for the fatal disease.

Reeves attended a special ceremony with Governor Whitman of New Jersey, USA, to see The Spinal Cord Research Act signed into law. The new law takes a $1 surcharge on motoring fines – estimated to generate an extra $3.2 million – and channels it into spinal cord research. Animal rights activists will have to think long and hard about whether to protest against such research. ■

Tiddles in Tinsel Town

From the days when Lassie was everyone's favourite dog to more modern-day successes such as Babe the pig or Willy the killer whale, animals have played a big part in the movies. You may not realise it, but today these animal actors are every bit as pampered as human celebs! The American Humane Association (AHA), an animal welfare organisation, has convinced Hollywood film studios to let it police the use of animals in film-making.

If you were concerned by the sight of the little dog being thrown from a third storey window in *There's Something About Mary*, never fear. The stunt was performed by a simple dummy dog, known in the trade as a 'stuffie', and the AHA was there to ensure no foul play. In fact, when the dog appears later in the film wearing a full-body cast, even this was done by making a lightweight, easily-removed fibre-glass cast, and spending weeks letting the dog actor become accustomed to wearing it.

AHA awards three levels of accreditation to films that have been made according to its guidelines. The lowest, 'Believed Acceptable', is awarded to well-made films when an AHA representative was not present on set. 'Acceptable' is awarded to films made properly, under AHA scrutiny. The highest grade,

Over the years, several collies found fame as Lassie.

awarded only to films made to tough animal welfare guidelines, permits the film-maker to add an 'End Credit Disclaimer' to the credits on the film, stating something to the effect that 'No animals were harmed in the making of this film'. ■

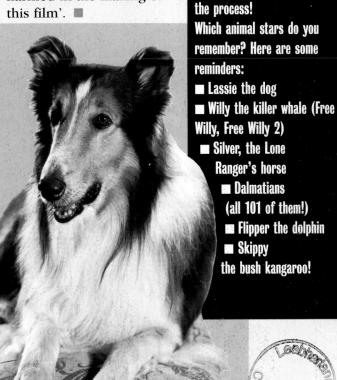

Hall of Fame

One of the biggest animal stars ever was Rin Tin Tin. He was a German shepherd dog that captured cinema-goers' hearts back in the 1920s – and saved a film studio in the process!

Which animal stars do you remember? Here are some reminders:
■ Lassie the dog
■ Willy the killer whale (Free Willy, Free Willy 2)
■ Silver, the Lone Ranger's horse
■ Dalmatians (all 101 of them!)
■ Flipper the dolphin
■ Skippy the bush kangaroo!

A Veggie Feast

Food Correspondent

Vegetarian products, including meat substitutes, are becoming a regular purchase in millions of homes. With well over 2 million vegetarians nationwide, and other consumers reaching for the Quorn for health or economy reasons, the only way is up.

Quorn was the first serious development of the market in the early 90s. It is a slightly spongy protein harvested from a special fungus, and has proved extremely adaptable as a meat substitute – indeed, some vegetarians find Quorn too similar to meat and refuse to touch it! But fungus protein has other advantages too – less than half the fat and none of the cholesterol of the meat it replaces.

We still consume approximately the same amount of meat as we did 15 years ago. But meat-eaters are far more likely to enjoy a veggie meal than they were back then. In a recent trial using a vegetarian 'Beanfeast' bolognese, 38% believed they were eating meat, compared to 46% who could tell the difference. With soya proteins and other meat substitutes costing anything from half to a fifth of the price of their meat alternative, could this be the beginning of the end for your local butcher?

Geoff Smallwood of the Meat and Livestock Commission doesn't think so: 'If sales of meat substitutes are improving, you've got to ask at whose expense? Meat sales haven't fallen – perhaps it's at the expense of baked beans'. ■

The popular Linda McCartney vegetarian range takes a stand against GM food.

Meat consumption up

Meat and Livestock Commission figures show that Britons now eat more meat than ever before – an average of 72kg each every year, compared to 44.4kg each in 1950. Beef consumption has fallen over the same period, replaced by a huge growth in the poultry market (from 2.5kg to 27.7kg each per year). ■

STRAWBERRY SURPRISE!

The surprise here is in the combination of ingredients. You might cringe while you're making it, but when you taste the results … *capow!* With not a whisker of an animal ingredient, this makes the perfect vegan starter.

- •3 punnets of strawberries
- •8 fresh basil leaves
- •45ml balsamic vinegar
- •90ml olive oil (extra-virgin)
- •Black pepper

Wash, dry and slice the strawberries, and place in the salad bowl. Cut the basil leaves into grass-blade slices and sprinkle on. Grind over some black pepper, and add the vinegar and oil. Toss the salad with care. Now amaze your tastebuds! ■

THOSE WE LEAVE BEHIND

As you make your travel plans this year, think carefully about what will happen to little Tiddles while you're away. Perhaps you know someone who can come to your house to feed a cat, but what if your pet needs more attention than a daily feed?

There are several things you can do. Kennels and catteries are well-established nationwide – just ask your vet to recommend a suitable place. No animal particularly enjoys being away from its own home, though, and you'll have a lot of cuddling to do to make up for it when you get back from your luxury break.

If the prospect of having your furry friend locked up while you're away leaves you feeling guilty, there are other alternatives. Least drastic is finding a reliable friend or relative to come and live in your home while you're away. This will give your pet companionship, and allow it to stay in its favourite place until you get home.

Do feel confident that your friends will look out for the animals. A family recently returned from holiday to find one of their cats near death. It had been shut in a bedroom for all their time away. The neighbours who had fed their cats in their absence had not even attempted to look for her!

If no friends or relatives fit the bill, you can hire a full-time pet-sitter; but watch out! They can be more expensive than your own holiday. ■

Going on holiday? Don't forget the cat...

Metal mutt

Sony Corporation may have made cruelty to pets a thing of the past, with its new toy 'dog', Aibo. The toy, a fully-functioning robot dog, can be programmed to fit your personal preferences. Needing only the occasional recharge, the pet makes a perfect Christmas present, when the alternative is an unwanted animal. ■

Firework protection

Owners of nervous pets have formed a lobby group, All Fireworks Frighten Animals, to try to have regulations over firework use changed. At present, all that dog and cat owners can do is draw the curtains, turn up the telly or radio and give their pet plenty of attention. ■

Herbal help

Evidence is growing that – alongside the usual veterinary procedures – herbal remedies have something to offer pets. The use of Aloe Vera gel, extracted from a cactus-like plant, has now been shown to speed the healing of cat and dog wounds by a third, leaving less scar tissue than more 'mainstream' antiseptics. ■

Dear Clare

Dear Clare,
I hope you can help. My cat Tigger used to be very cuddly and friendly. Now he won't come when I call, and sometimes runs away when I go to stroke him. He's been spayed, and the vet says that there's nothing wrong with him. What can I do?
Felix Lover

Dear Felix,
Don't worry! Tigger's just grown up a bit. Cats can become more independent as they get older, but this doesn't mean that they will stop being your friend. In some ways, it's a compliment – he's comfortable enough around you that he doesn't have to 'act the kitten' any more to butter you up! One tip might encourage him back into your arms: don't make him feel like you're pursuing him. Cats are sensitive to being watched, and often slowly blink and look away when they're trying to make friends. When Tigger looks at you, try blinking, turning your head away, and then turning back. He might reward your politeness with a cuddle! ■

Ecotourism
THE SHAPE OF THINGS TO COME

The travel sector is booming, and the fastest area of growth is in Ecotourism. But is Ecotourism really helping, or is it just another marketing trick?

The Travel Editor

The Ecotourism Society defines the sector as 'purposeful travel to natural areas, to understand the culture and natural history of the environment, taking care not to alter the integrity of the ecosystem, while producing economic opportunities that make the conservation of natural resources beneficial to local people'. Got that?

Understandably, not many tour companies manage to hit every one of these bases, but there are some very good schemes to choose from nonetheless.

Tourism was almost entirely responsible for saving the mountain gorillas of Rwanda from extinction. The country's Parc des Volcans, established by the famous amateur naturalist Diane Fossey, charges $170 per day per visitor. The money raised has transformed the great ape's prospects, allowing the government to pay farmers who previously may have illegally hunted them, employing them instead as wardens and guides.

APE SAVED

Sadly, too many such tours rely on Western airlines, hotel chains and tour staff for the proceeds to go where they are most needed – to local conservation projects. Too many tourists in one area can also create extra problems – litter, disruption to an ecosystem and damage from supply needs such as the burning of wood for cooking and hot water.

Alta Floresta, a Brazilian highland town, is the glowing example that shows how ecotourism should function. Alongside the educational experience tourists enjoy, the ecotourism centre devotes considerable energy to community work, ensuring that local people are involved in the management of both the ecosystem and of the tourism business. Perhaps it's not quite as much fun as Disneyworld, but you can go home with a certain amount of pride… ■

A mountain gorilla with its baby in the Parc des Volcans.

The Ecotourist's Choice

Here is a selection of tourist destinations where ecotourists can find excellent packages that highlight the aspect of responsible tourism and show how local communities can benefit from the activities undertaken by travellers:

- Ecuador
- Isle of Skye
- Kenya
- New Zealand
- Peru
- Portugal
- South Africa
- Tanzania and Zanzibar
- Trinidad and Tobago.

About 1200km west of Portugal, in the middle of the Atlantic Ocean, lies the group of islands known as the Azores, a haven for humans and wildlife alike. If you're a fan of whales and dolphins, here is a great place to come for some extraordinary close encounters.

Whale-watchers have a close encounter with an orca (or killer whale).

Whale of a time!

The Azores has a long association with whales, but until 1981, when the Convention on International Trade in Endangered Species (CITES) extended protection to them, the beautiful creatures were seen only as a source of oils and cheap fertiliser.

The last whale was taken here commercially in 1984, since when income from whale watching tourists has replaced the whale harvesting economy. Tourist dollars also finance vital whale conservation work.

Serge Viallelle, a Frenchman, set up the Espaco Talassa centre on the island of Pico in 1989. The centre conducts serious cetacean research and education, besides offering charter boats to take groups and individuals whale watching. With their network of lookouts in radio contact with the boats, and an underwater microphone for eavesdropping on whalesong, you are almost guaranteed a cetacean encounter with these experienced crews.

THAR SHE BLOWS!

In 1999 over 17 different species of cetacea were spotted on their trips, including dolphins, orcas (killer whales) and pilot whales. If you're moderately lucky, you may see a sperm whale, a rare sight in most other whale-watching spots around the world. An encounter with a 20 metre, 70 tonne male sperm whale must surely rate amongst the most memorable holiday experiences ever!

The Azores are reached by changing planes at Lisbon, Portugal, flying on to the international airport on Faial Island. Would-be whale-watchers can contact Espaco Talassa, Rua do Saco 9930, Larges do Pico, Azores. Tel: 00-351-292-672010 Fax: 00-351-292-672617, e-mail: viallelle@espacotalassa.com and check out their web site on www.espacotalassa.com ■

WHALING RETURNS

Despite the world-wide ban on commercial whaling introduced in the 1980s, Iceland returned to hunting small numbers of minke whales for study in 2003. Greenpeace warned Icelanders that tourists would stay away in protest so resumed whaling would be 'economic suicide'. Tourism, however, increased by 16%. In Norway too, where some whaling was re-introduced in 2003, holiday makers appear to be ignoring Greenpeace's concerns and whale-watching tourism is flourishing ■

The Long March

Here are some key moments in the development of animal welfare activity around the world:

1822
British MP Richard Martin sponsored the Animal Protection Act, which outlawed cruelty to cattle, horses and sheep. It was the world's first ever animal welfare law.

1824
The Society for the Prevention of Cruelty to Animals (SPCA) was established, with the backing of Richard Martin MP and William Wilberforce MP. It was the first law enforcement agency in the UK, securing 149 convictions in its first year.

1829
The newly-founded Royal Zoological Society took charge of the royal menagerie, held at the Tower of London, establishing what was to become London Zoo.

1840
Queen Victoria gave her blessing to the SPCA, granting it Royal status (RSPCA).

1859
On the Origin of Species by Natural Selection by Charles Darwin was published. His research revealed that humans and animals are related, which first raised the possibility that animals might be seen as equal to humans.

1935
American Animal Welfare League of Chicago establishes the city's first animal shelter.

1961
The World Wildlife Fund (WWF) established to conserve endangered species and their habitats.

1969
International Fund for Animal Welfare established with the immediate aim to end the harvesting of baby seals in Canada, quickly extending its objectives to end cruelty against other animals around the world.

1973
The Convention on International Trade in Endangered Species is signed by 80 countries, to stamp out the trade in endangered species.

1975
Animal Liberation by Peter Singer published. The book laid out a strong argument in favour of animal rights, inspiring many more people to become involved in animal rights campaigns.

1980
People for the Ethical Treatment of Animals (PeTA) established to persuade people and governments that animals are not ours to eat, wear, experiment on or use for entertainment.

1983
EEC imposes first ban on seal products, to run for two years. The ban was later made permanent.

1991
South Korea passes its first Animal Protection Act in response to NGO campaigns.

1992
New Fellowship established at Oxford University to study animal welfare concerns.

1996
Wild Mammals Protection Act brought wild animals as well as pets under the protection of anti-cruelty legislation.

1998
Philippines passes the Animal Welfare Act. Amongst other achievements, it put an end to the cruel treatment of dogs bred for their meat.

2003
Germany changes constitution to recognise animals. Lawyers disagree over whether this gives them equal rights. ■

Feeding the bears at London Zoo, 1873.

Is it time for the sight of horse and hounds to become a thing of the past?

IS HUNTING A SPORT?

We **roughly define sports as any physical activity pursued** just for exercise or pleasure. Does hunting with hounds qualify? Or, for that matter, any of the other so-called 'blood' sports?

The Sports Editor

For the majority of hunt followers, the main attraction of the hunt is to test their riding skills, and the training of their horse. In this respect, hunting is more like accepted sports, such as show jumping, than other blood sports such as shooting and fishing.

If the pleasure of hunting comes from the chase, drag hunts (where a person takes the place of the fox) would be a logical compromise. But while this should make hunting acceptable to the majority, it would break with 300 years of the sport's rituals and culture. Would the sport survive?

Shooting and fishing have similar ethical problems: is the pleasure really in the kill rather than the activity? But these arguably less brutal of country pursuits seem safe from controls. As Tony Blair has put it, 'there will be no ban on the country pursuits of shooting and fishing.'

Most MPs are against hunting for sport. Indeed, defenders of foxhunting seem to agree. It is rare for pro-hunting campaigners to argue that hunting is fun. They prefer to defend it as a means of controlling vermin, or as a cornerstone of the rural economy. ■

Order!

In 1699, a new law proposed in the British House of Commons was defeated by ten votes. John Evelyn, a diarist, tells us that the law's supporters failed to turn up because they were too busy watching a tiger being baited by dogs. ■

Fox pop

In the heyday of foxhunting in the 18th century, foxes came so close to extinction that they had to be imported from the continent. Known as 'bagmen', the foxes were traded at Leadenhall Market, London. Hunts from around the country bought the 'bagmen' here and took them back to the hunt's kennels, where they would be kept until needed for the chase. ■

Beastly Brit

Bulldogs, one of the popular images of the British personality, were specifically bred to bait bulls, an entertainment enjoyed by Queen Elizabeth I. ■

Uneatable

Oscar Wilde, the 19th-century writer and wit, described a huntsman as 'the unspeakable in full pursuit of the uneatable'. ■

Trainer confesses to drugs charge

Steroids give horses added strength in racing, but have dangerous side-effects.

New drugs test reveals steroid use in horse-racing

Top **Australian trainer Anthony Cummings admitted administering** anabolic steroids to 45 horses in his care in a special court held to investigate the case.

Mr Cummings, the son of the legendary Melbourne Cup winner Bart Cummings, claimed that he believed the drugs he had administered contained only amino acids.

He denied knowing that they in fact contained trenbolone, a drug licensed for use in beef cattle to boost health and improve appetite (see Mafia beef, page 8). Tests for trenbolone in racehorses were only introduced last year.

HORSE POWER

Trenbolone is a member of a group of drugs classed as anabolic steroids. This is the same type of drug that is banned for human consumption. It improves muscle-tone and power, but can cause circulatory problems, including heart attacks and strokes. Athletes are routinely tested for traces of steroids and banned from competitions if tests prove positive. The drug can be equally dangerous for horses. ■

(see Mafia beef, page 8).

GAMBLING WITH LIVES

Organisers of the National Hunt are well prepared to face any disruption of the Grand National race by animal welfare protestors, after skirmishes in previous years. The three-day race meet, with a reputation as one of the world's finest steeplechases, has resorted to employing several hundred security staff to ensure that demonstrators fail to disrupt the main event.

Karen Harvey, of Action to Abolish the Grand National, claimed that up to 250 horses are killed each year in National Hunt races over large obstacles. 'It's not like an injured jockey who ends up in hospital with gifts of chocolate; the horses end up on a dog's dinner plate,' she said. Racegoers were, in general, unsympathetic to demonstrators outside the course. As one simply put it, 'Horses love racing.' ■

POLLUTION? YES, PLEASE!

Clean water puts a stop to big catches in River Trent.

Stocks of freshwater fish have plummeted in one of the UK's most famous coarse fishing rivers, the Trent. The National Coarse Fishing Championship, traditionally held along the banks of the Trent, has been cancelled due to lack of fish.

Why has the Trent's abundance of roach and other popular anglers' fish disappeared? Did the sewage works poison the river? Have farmers used too many nitrates on nearby fields? Is a factory illegally dumping toxic chemicals here?

The answer, according to fishermen and the Environment Agency, is the exact opposite – since Severn Trent Water Company invested £20m in improving its Stoke Bardolph sewage works, the river has become too clean!

The lack of sewage and other muck in the water leaves fish exposed to predators, such as cormorants. The lack of organic compounds in the water is also thought to lead to a loss of feeding materials for many small fish.

Martin Stark, the Environment Agency's fisheries manager for the Midlands, said 'the clean up has made the river poorer in fish in some ways'. But as a local fishing tackle retailer, Tim Aplin, asks, 'What do we do about it? We don't want to make the river dirty again, do we?' ■

WELL SAVED!

David Seaman, Arsenal keeper, has adopted a dog from the Mayhew Animal Home. Seaman told the Mayhew's in-house magazine, Animal Rescue, that he was 'not interested in forking out loads of money for a pedigree dog ... we prefer to give an unwanted animal a chance'.

ANIMAL GLOVER!

The very wealthy goalie and his partner, Debbie, had to have their home checked out by a Home Visitor. As soon as they were given the thumbs up, Maxi moved in, rapidly becoming part of the family. A charity auction of a pair of David's goal-keeping gloves recently raised £500 for the Mayhew. ■

David Seaman has his hands full with love-able mutt Maxi

WHO'S WHO

Here are just a few of the pressure groups and charities devoted to the cause of animal welfare, although often with very different views as to how to this cause can be best supported. Whatever their position, you can contact them for more information or visit their websites.

■ **Born Free Foundation**
Works to return captive animals to the wild, and conserve endangered species. 3 Grove House, Foundry Lane, Horsham, West Sussex RH13 5PL http://www.bornfree.org.uk/

■ **Compassion in World Farming**
Researches animal welfare in farming and lobbies for improvements. 5a Charles Street, Petersfield, Hants GU32 3EH http://www.ciwf.co.uk/

■ **Humane Research Trust**
Aims to replace animal experiments with alternatives. http://www.btinternet.com/~shawweb/hrt/

■ **League Against Cruel Sports**
Campaigns to ban hunting, shooting and fishing. 83/7 Union Street, London SE1 1SG   http://lacs.org.uk/

■ **People for the Ethical Treatment of Animals (PeTA)**
Founded in 1980 to establish and protect the rights of all animals. PeTA Europe Ltd, PO Box 3169, London SW18 4WJ

http://www.peta-online.org/

■ **Research Defence Society**
Advises on the advantages of animal experimentation, to counter the claims of anti-vivisection groups. 25 Shaftesbury Avenue, London W1D 7EG http://www.rds-online.org.uk

■ **RSPCA**
The world's oldest animal charity. Causway, Horsham, Sussex RH12 1HG http://www.rspca.org.uk/

■ **Vegetarians' International Voice for Animals**
Animal rights campaign with an international focus. 8 York Court, Wilder Street, Bristol, BS2 8QH http://www.viva.org.uk/

■ **Whale and Dolphin Conservation Society**
Campaigns to aid cetacean (that is, whales and dolphins) welfare. http://www.wdcs.org

■ **World Wide Fund for Nature (WWF)**
Campaigns internationally to protect endangered species and habitats. Panda House, Wyside Park, Godalming, Surrey GU7 1XR   http://www.wwf.org/

■ **Royal Society of Provention of Cruelty to Animals Australia (RSPCA)**
Working to prevent cruelty to animals. 201 Rookwood Rd, Yagoona NSW 2199;PO Box 34, Yagoona NSW 2199 http://www.rspca.org.au

■ **Save-A-Dog Scheme Inc**
Saves dogs from being put down at dog pounds and animal rescue homes. Adopt-a-dog! PO Box 78, East Caulfield, Melbourne VIC 3145 http://www.alterriermotives.com.au/save-a-dog.hmtl

■ **Wildlife Information and Rescue Service (WIRES)**
The largest wildlife rescue group in Australia. PO Box 260, Forestville, NSW 2087 WIRES Rescue Phone Numbers: NSW COUNTRY 1800 641 188; SYDNEY (02) 8977 3333 http://www.wires.webcentral.com.au

■ **World Society for the Preservation of Animals (WSPA)**
Campaigns internationally on animal welfare issues.
http://www.wspa.org.au
http://www.wspa.org.nz ■

Note to parents and teachers
Every effort has been made by the Publishers to ensure that these websites are suitable for children; that they are of the highest educational value, and that they contain noinappropriate or offensive material.However, because of the nature of the Internet, it is impossible to guarantee that the contents of these sites will not be altered. We strongly advise that Internet access is supervised by a responsible adult.

YOUR VIEWS ON THE NEWS

The Animal News doesn't just want to give you its views on the news. It wants you, its readers, to talk about the issues too. Here are some questions to get you going:

■ Should hunting be banned? What about shooting and fishing?
■ How influenced are you by issues of animal welfare when you go shopping for clothes or food? Does labelling affect your choices?

■ In what ways are environmental issues linked with animals?
■ What can we do to stop people being cruel to animals?
■ Do you think that standards of animal welfare should be the same all around the world? If so, how could this be achieved?
■ What do you think about vivisection? Is it ever justifiable?
■ How do you think education can help promote animal welfare?

■ Do you think we should talk about animal rights or animal welfare? Why?
■ Are zoos good for animal welfare? What about circuses?
■ Would you like a career working with animals? If so, what sort?
■ If you wanted to raise money for an animal welfare charity, how would you set about it?
■ What problems do you think ecotourism could create?
■ Is racing cruel?

WHAT'S WHAT

Here's *The Animal News'* quick reference aid explaining some terms you'll have come across in its pages.

■ **activist** A person who expresses their political beliefs through active participation, including protests, lobbying politicians, publicity stunts or occasional violence.

■ **animal rights** Those rights thought by some to be due to animals just as they are to people, recognising their equal status as living, sensitive beings.

■ **animal welfare** Looking after an animal's basic needs – food, shelter and healthcare – and ensuring it is not treated by humans with cruelty or experiences unnecessary suffering.

■ **BSE** Bovine Spongiform Encephalopathy – a cow's disease of the brain which leaves it, literally, looking like a sponge. Broke out in British beef herds in the late 1980s, and thought to have caused a similar brain disease in humans through the eating of infected beef.

■ **bankruptcy** Companies or businessmen who cannot pay their debts go into bankruptcy. A bankrupt's possessions are sold to clear as many of the debts as possible.

■ **biodiversity** The range of animals and plants found in one place. A broad biodiversity indicates a healthy environment (see also *ecosystem*).

■ **blood sports** Traditional activities people enjoy which involve catching or killing animals, such as hunting foxes and shooting birds.

■ **cash crops** Plants grown by farmers for sale rather than for their own food supply.

■ **cetacean** Any sea-living mammal of fish-like appearance, including whales, dolphins and porpoises.

■ **civil rights** A group of claims to personal freedom all citizens can demand from the authorities. Arguments over civil rights often deal with the unfair treatment of groups of citizens, e.g. ethnic minorities.

■ **Convention on International Trade in Endangered Species (CITES)** An agreement signed by most countries to try to stop rare animals being killed or sold for money.

■ **damages** Money the law requires a wrong-doer to pay to victims to make up for the harm caused.

■ **dissection** Cutting open a dead plant or animal to study its structure.

■ **distemper** A group of diseases, especially viruses and fevers, affecting animals.

■ **ecosystem** A network of plants and animals which support and depend on each other for survival.

■ **enteritis** An inflammation of the intestine (part of the digestive system) caused by various diseases.

■ **environment** The physical processes and objects which support life.

■ **Environment Agency, the** The UK government department which looks after the environment.

■ **ethics** Ideas about what is right or wrong.

■ **European Union (EU)** The group of European countries which has agreed to work together by obeying a set of rules which deal with everything from farming practices to civil rights.

■ **food chain** A series of plants and creatures in which each feeds on the next, e.g. plant, insect, frog, bird.

■ **genetically modified (GM)** Plants and animals altered to make them more useful to humans by changing a particular gene or genes.

■ **hormones** Naturally-occurring chemicals in the body with a variety of jobs. Hormones can be copied by scientists and used to change the way a body works.

■ **humane** Treating people or animals with respect, causing the minimum stress or pain.

■ **malaria** A disease of the blood carried by mosquitoes and transmitted when they bite. Malaria causes a severe fever and, if not treated, can lead to brain damage or death.

■ **malnutrition** The damage to health resulting from starvation or a poor diet.

■ **NGO (Non-governmental Organisation)** Groups, including charities, which perform socially-beneficial tasks but are not directly a part of government.

■ **neuter** To remove the ovaries or testicles of an animal to stop it reproducing.

■ **organic** Food production which replaces industrial fertilisers and pesticides with chemicals derived from plants or animals.

■ **parasites** Organisms which live on and take all their food from the body of a larger 'host' animal or plant.

■ **Parkinson's disease** A disease which causes the sufferer to shake and lose control of limbs.

■ **processed food** Any pre-prepared or 'ready-meal' food, where the seller has combined ingredients to create it.

■ **rabies** A virus transmitted by saliva from animal bites, causing thirst, an inability to swallow and eventual death. Can be treated if caught early.

■ **steroids** Group of drugs used to boost muscle growth. Illegal for athletes, steroids are used in some countries to improve beef production.

■ **United Nations (UN)** The organisation of all the countries of the world, which attempts to maintain peace and resolve global issues such as the environment through debate and diplomatic agreements.

■ **vegan** A person who chooses to eat no animal produce, including meat, dairy products, eggs and – by some definitions – honey.

■ **vivisection** The use of animals in experiments, typically for human medical science, but also for testing the safety of consumer products.

■ **xenotransplantation** Using the organs from one species in organ donor surgery for another species, e.g. using GM-pig organs for humans with heart or kidney failure.

INDEX